yes, i am.

a transformational coloring
book consciously crafted
to support you in being
your very best you ever (yet).
and to laugh. a lot.

dani katz

for the new p.* superheroes

* paradigm

about this super rad book

adapted from the <u>i am calendar</u>, <u>yes, i am</u> is a transformational coloring book designed to prompt, prod, beckon, cajole, guide and support you in being your very best you ever (yet).

<u>yes, i am</u> was hand-drawn, with every line rendered in the tonglen spirit of giving + taking, in service to a happy, healthy harmonious humanity; and a balanced, thriving planet earth.

daily reading, coloring, sharing + participating is encouraged. and fun.

x o d k

just as the <u>i am calendar</u>
featured a different "i am"
theme each month, the <u>i
am coloring book</u> is divided
into twelve different "i am"
chapters.

"i am" are the most powerful
words in all the mystical
traditions. encoded in these
words is the transformative
power of the ~~universe~~.

MULTIVERSE.

use 'em wisely, kiddos.

i am...

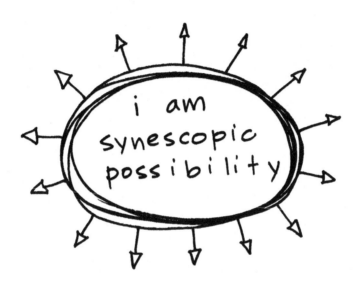

synescopic

[sin-uh-skō-pik] adj, every moment access to every potentiality that is, was or will be.

use it in place of "limitless."

"

"

_____

(without having to utter "limit" in the process.)

yay for lexicon expansion!

humans are brilliant + innovative | you are human $\therefore$ you are brilliant + innovative

 $\boxed{\therefore}$ means "therefore" in math.

envision

invent

explore

imagine. a lot.

investigate the edges.
expand them.

known reality

novelty
rocks.

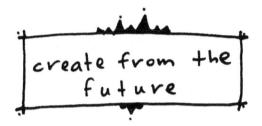

create from the future

jar o' future

if you can imagine it...

...you have already manifested it

(on some dimension).

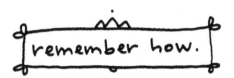

remember how.

do this:

1. connect to your dream future.

2. sprinkle that vibration all over your now.

dream biggest

did you know...

prrr.

...a cat's purr vibrates at the same vibrational frequency as unconditional love?

540 hz

·kitty love
·hope
·willingness
·shame
·fear

prrr

how wide will
your ♡ open?

dare
yourself
to find out.

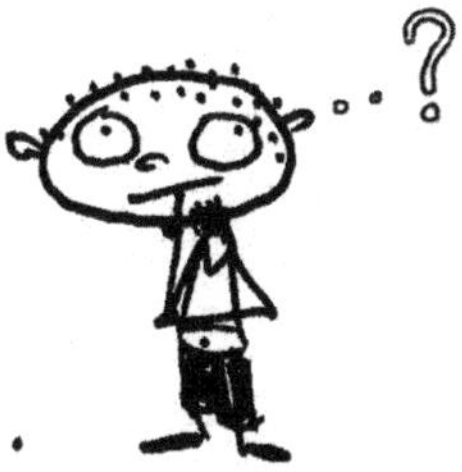

the next time someone
tells you they love you...

~ stop ~

...and let your every fractal
cell soak up the message.

i bow to your stinky, muddy dog paws, oh great guru of unconditional love.

i am unconditional love
for myself + others.
al(l)ways.

```
love up
  your
insides.
```

a sampling of love morsels:

- chocolate
- figs
- coconut cream
- strawberries
- cheremoya
- fresh squeezed orange juice
- cashew butter

hurray!

♥ + now =

do this:

remember (often) how
massively much the
multiverse loves
your guts.

remembering

thank your body
for all the wonderful
things it does to
keep you alive +
move you through
time-space.

thank you, belly.
i ♡ you,
belly.

thank you, hands!!!

breathe deeply
+
consciously
every day.

early to bed
early to rise
makes for an
optimized
ninja superhero
you.

do this:

move.
sweat.
breathe.
repeat.

what is your favorite
way to exercise?

rebounding!

squats

kung fu.

racquetball!

do that. a lot.

eat : ☐ organic
☐ whole
☐ local
☐ fresh
☒ all of the above

honey

herbs

ginger

let thy food
be thy medicine

lemon

turmeric

salt

i am optimized well-being personified.
say this. with feeling.

take
the
stairs

squatting makes for ergonomically awesome pooping.

engage
your
core.

drink more,
better,
wetter water.

in fact, take a sip <u>right now.</u>

filtered
alkaline
mineralized
spring!
spun
blessed

— thanks, folate. thanks, vitamin k

thanks, parsnip!

thank your veggies (and your other food stuff) for their every optimized nutrient.

thanks, quinoa.

— thank you, non-gmo corn.

there has never been, nor will there ever be again, anyone quite like **you**.

everyone has their own truth
based on their own values. do not
discount anyone else's truth based
on <u>your</u> values.

1. family
2. comfort
3. honesty

1. evolution
2. compassion
3. freedom

1. adventure
2. service
3. cheese

forgive your
every perceived
transgression.

speak your truth.
even if your voice
shakes.

everyone can dance.
how does your body
like to move?

on my toes

with my
face +
my feet.
minimalist, yo.

down
low while shakin'
my booty.

this moment.

this orientation of your
body on this spinning
planet, orbiting the sun,
hurtling through deep
space.

this configuration of
cells + bone + blood + dna
is absolutely unique...

who are you right now?

actively engage your
s h a d o w s
so as to transmute
them into gifts that
make the world more
w o n d e r f u l.

track your
behavior
patterns.

without a shred
of judgment

· cranky when
  hungry.
· warm + open
  in the morning.
· bratty to
  mom when
  she pushes.

is
your opinion
really
your opinion?

you know
because you
figured it out
on your own—
because it
wasn't
indoctrinated
upon you.

i think so.
how can i
know for
sure?

radiate your own
magical frequency
as a gift to the world.

human incarnation
is a growth game.
allow yourself your
path + all the lessons
it brings you.

say/know/embody this:

what if your freckles are really a coded message from the universe?

intuition
is an internal
compass that
points you
toward   truth

intuition
tutorial

how to connect with your
internal "yes" and "no":

1. sit quietly.

2. say "i am a dinosaur."

3. feel that in your body.

4. say "i am a human being."

5. feel that in your body.

#5 = yes
#3 = no

be you.

of our reality
is unseen.

create intentionally

thank you, tea, for 
infusing
me with
wisdom
and
inspiration.

eau de cosmos

magic tools:
- elements
- plants
- minerals
- symbols
- words
- animals
- colors
- your imagination

do this:

track your synchronicities

wow. i keep seeing threes. i wonder what they mean...

animal spirits carry powerful messages. and magic.

bugs, too!

look up the properties of the spirit totems that cross your path.

then, contemplate accordingly.

tapped in.

connect with the elements

listen to the wind

be alone in nature.

track the stars, and
mind the moon cycles.

connect to your intuition.

handy-dandy intuition to english dictionary

chills: truth
love
recognition

anxiety: danger

heavy ♡/ belly issues: negativity

throat tingles: need to express/ communicate

embrace
the
unknown.

you are _____
responsible for
your reality.
_____

a. 40%.
b. sorta
c. 100%.
d. none of the
   above

yay! that
means i can
make my
reality even
radder than
it already is!!!

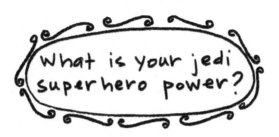

What is your jedi superhero power?

word-nerd. duh.

S.h.o.e. super heart-open empath.

pattern recognition.

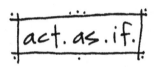

act.as.if.

firm handshakes
are sexy.

☐ say
☐ know
☐ embody
☒ all of the above
            this:

has no place in
a superstar's
lexicon

it's <u>your</u> job to acknowledge <u>your</u> awesomeness + <u>your</u> unique genius.

it is? but, isn't that what friends are for?

no. that's codependence, not confidence.

sadie, you are a fantastic listener, and you are rockin' that dress. you. are. rad.

do this:

compliment yourself. (+ oThers) daily. often.

never complain.
never explain.

own your greatness.

also on it.

everything happens
precisely when it's
meant to happen.

wear your fanciest favorite everything just because.

now is as special an occasion as any.

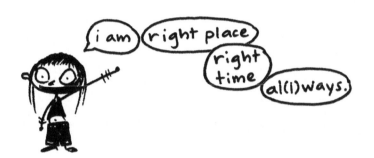

there is only
one moment
now

now
past
future
are you reflecting on the past?
are you projecting onto the future?
come back to this gorgeous now.

silence your mind.

connect with your
sensory experience:

- what are you seeing?

- tune into the sound-
scape - the buzzes,
the voices, the hums,
the honks ... listen.

- take a big ol' sniff.
whaddya smell?

- check in with your
left elbow. what's
going on with that guy?

tomorrow
will
n e v e r
get here.

time ≠ linear

try to
act like a
grown-up

birth   puberty   wither + ache   death

despite all appearances + experiences to the contrary, time is not, in fact, linear.

be mindful of
the future you
are seeding...

do this: hang out in the timeless realms...

* make art
* play a sport
* chill in nature
* connect w/ other beings
* make stuff
* pick your face

don't do this, regardless of how fun it is.

patience,
little one.

i am a healthy, balanced, thriving planet earth.

schumann resonance

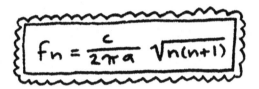

$$f_n = \frac{c}{2\pi a} \sqrt{n(n+1)}$$

the frequency of the
earth's breath pattern

i ♥ you, cool breeze.

the earth isn't just
our home planet,
it is an intelligent,
living consciousness.
with this in mind,
love her up with your
thoughts + intentions.

thank
you
pacha
mama.

turn off the
water while
you shave your legs.

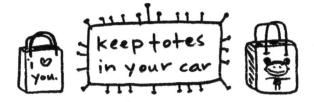

thank you,
photosynthesis.

we ♥ you, polar bears.

unplug the
stuff you're not
using

mend hol(e)y socks
+ sweaters instead
of buying new ones.

do this: pick up the trash in your path.

no matter. you
have eyes to see
+ hands to grasp,
+ you are just as
responsible for
your planet's well-
being as <u>we all are</u>.

but, i'm
not the
one who
littered.

recycle.
everything you
possibly can.

cut up
old t-shirts
to use as
dust rags!

almond
butter
no
more

bring your own
containers for
takeaway food
+ beverages.

tend a garden.

we are, all of us,
earthlings.

i am
abundance

lakshmi

hindu goddess
of
abundance

the universe provides.

the extent to which you
trust this is the extent
to which you receive
a b u n d a n c e.

whoa.

...number ninety-one: opposable thumbs; number ninety-two: climate control; number ninety-three...

i acknowledge kindness
laughter + magic as the
highest + most supreme
currency

prosperity is
an orientation
of consciousness.

say know feel embody this:

i radiate prosperity.

money likes to circulate.

what feelings does this symbol
inspire in your body?

pros·per·i·ty : n.
having what you
need when you
need it.

wait. i
think
that
means
i'm already
prosperous.

word,
grass·
hopper.

create (in) abundance.

prosperity infuses my
every word and line.

banish these statements from your story + your mind.

i'm broke

i can't afford it.

they only render you powerless + victim-y.

better:

no, thank you.

the "why" doesn't matter.

cultivate receptivity

how?

- listen deeper, longer, more
- ask for support
- resist the urge to fill the empty space
- graciously avail yourself to compliments, well-wishes, blessings + offerings
- allow space for spontanaeity + surprise
- allow, allow, allow

allow.
avail.
receive.

describe your very best
version of **yourself**.

i am happy +
inspired + warm
+ loving + radiant.

no mind.
no "i".
just bliss.

intend
+
embody
that you.

i vibrate at the frequency of :

☐ genius
☐ compassion
☐ love
☐ amazing
☐ magnificent
☒ all of the above

how do you inhabit your body when you are at your very best?

shoulders back →

chin up.

feet wide

do this:

take that posture before you leave the house every day.

honor the reflections
before you. every one.

ask others to define
their terms to optimize
communication + amplify
understanding.

how are
you
defining
"genius"?

*a natural
creative
uniqueness
rooted in
unconditional
love

*richard rudd, the gene keys

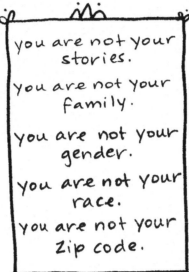

you are not your stories.
You are not your family.
You are not your gender.
You are not your race.
You are not your Zip code.

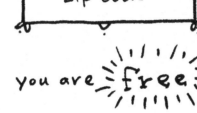

you are free

90210

grow your emotional intelligence.

- take responsibility
- set boundaries
- communicate clearly, kindly + consistently in real time.
- open your heart.

be brave! you can do it!

f*@k
anti-
aging

optimization

is saner, and
way more fun.

bless your water.

i love you, water. thank you for infusing me with good great wonderful optimizing mojo.

— i am an intelligent living consciousness!

your blessings infuse me with their energetic frequencies, which you get to drink, thus blessing yourself, too!

— whoa. rad. on it.

activate
your

dna

how?

by feeling
good +
joyful.

what are your favorite
ways to express?

1. dance
2. draw
3. hula-hoop

do those
things.
a lot.

an optimized
being is an
expressed
being.

embody
your
ideal
outcome.

intend your
optimized
awesomeness.
aloud.
every day.
with feeling.

do this: connect with _yourself_ every day. make it a ritual.

some methods include

* cooking
♥ walking
⊙ meditating
△ exercising
✳ being outside
✿ cloud-watching
✾ gardening

on it.

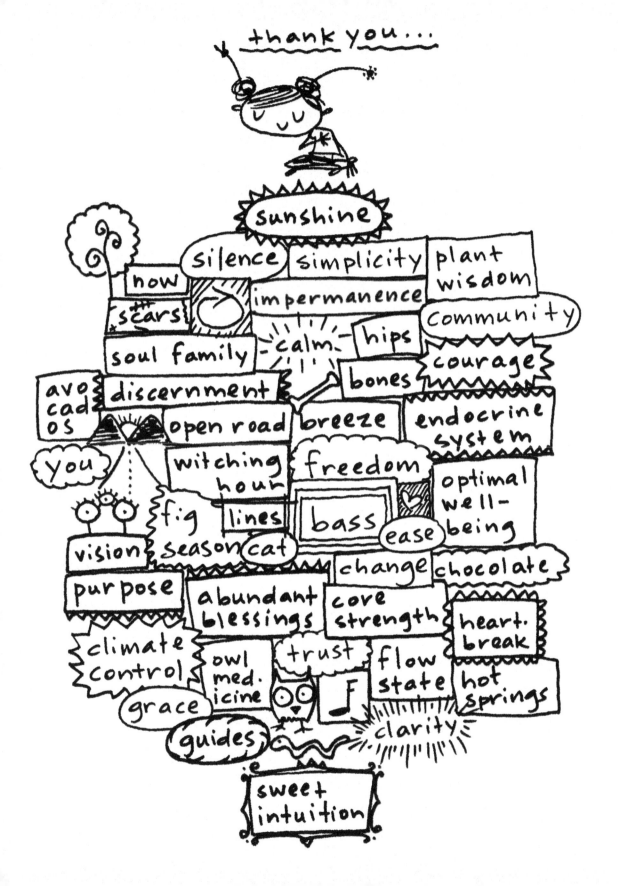

one
consciousness.
many
meat suits.

empaths feel other people's
feelings in their own bodies

uh-oh.
Someone's
barfing
somewhere.

dear empath...

be sure to ask yourself:

is this my feeling?

handy-dandy empath tools:

- cloak
- grounding cord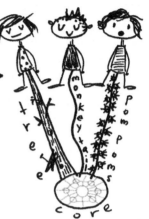
- cord-cutting blade
- golden grid
- saltwater (bath, ocean, tears)
- rosewater

(of the earth)

note: ~~some~~ lots of these you use in your imagination

you are part of the original thought.

yes, you.

did you know that all human
beings are connected
through an invisible matrix
of information, influence +
memory called the
morphogenetic field?

everything is energy.

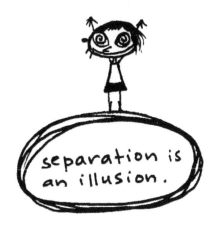

we are **one**:
☐ heart
☐ mind
☐ being
☒ all of the above

your _____ lightens
the species' load.

☐ joy
☐ laughter
☐ love
☐ evolution
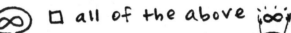
☐ all of the above

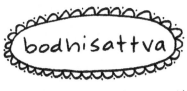

bodhisattva

one who walks the path of enlightenment, but delays buddhahood until all sentient beings wake up.

whoa.
bad ass.

| tonglen | : ° ° | tibetan buddist practice of giving and taking |

how to tonglen:

1. inhale others' suffering
2. exhale happiness + wellbeing to all sentient beings

taking

giving

every line
a giving
+ taking

it takes a ~~village.~~ species.

dani katz is a
human being.
she writes.
she draws.
she dances.
she lives in her
native los angeles.
she loves water,
semi-colons + you.

Made in the USA
Las Vegas, NV
09 June 2021